RENTAL PROPERTY INVESTING

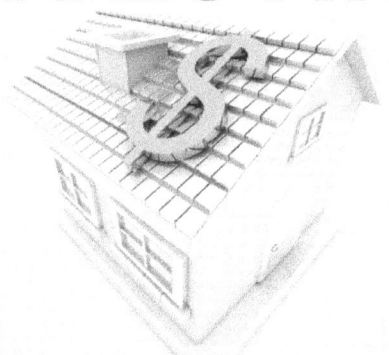

Creating Income By Eliminating The Noise Of A Loud Industry

COLE GRAHAM

COLE GRAHAM

Rental Property Investing

Creating Income by Eliminating the Noise of a Loud Industry

Cole Graham

ISBN: 1983555851
ISBN-13: 978-1983555855

CONTENTS

COLE GRAHAM

INTRODUCTION

The world of real estate within reach, the sky's the limit and you just cannot wait another year to get started. I'm with you 100%. I've always been someone who just wanted to dive right in and figure it out as I went along. However, over time I've learned that this strategy isn't always the best one and at times can even be the most expensive one.

There's a time and a place to take action. Can I teach you every single thing there is to know about real estate, absolutely not, and here's why. Properties are like humans, every single one is different. I don't care if you are looking to purchase a house in a neighborhood were every third house has the same floor plan. I assure you that one house has more nails then the other. I promise you that every wall in the house is not at 90 degrees, meaning each wall is a little off from what was on the blueprint. The same people did not live in each house, and they did not get the same repair company to fix any issues. Therefore, it is literally impossible to give you every answer to every possible scenario that is out there simply because each house is different. Let me ask you this, can you raise every child in the world the exact same way? Nope, I mean you might have some rules that are applied the same, but kids all have their own personalities.

What this book can do is give you some very helpful information in making right decisions for yourself. I can give you some strategies and idea to think about that can help your put together a game plan and some criteria to help reduce the risk of making a poor investment. In this book, I have simplified purchasing a rental property. I have simplified what you need to look for, described the difference in single and multi-family properties and how you can benefit from both. I will also go over some strategies and financial option to help understand what types of options you have available.

Real estate is an industry with some many different levels. You could start out buy simply purchasing a single-family rental and find you love it and want to expand. Expanding is as easy as purchasing another single-family home or purchase a multi-family home. If you want to expand even more, put some money aside you've made and put a down payment on a commercial property with 15-20 units. You can scale up at any time if you find it to be enjoyable.

I strongly believe that once you have read through this book you will have all the information you need to purchase your first rental property.

Thank you for downloading this book.

Let's get started.

1 KNOW THE BASICS

Before we get into money, strategies and becoming successful in real estate, let's start simple. By simple, I mean things that need to be considered, but can easily be overlooked. These certain things are often overlooked by newbies who really don't know what they are doing, but are excited to just purchase their first house. They can also be passed over by a veteran who is just a little too confident, may have a little too much on their plate or get caught with their pants down.

Below is a list of things that I consider to be simple, maybe obvious, but cannot be overlooked:

Type of Property

You need to ask yourself what type of property do you want to get start off with. Whether it be single-family, a duplex, multi-family, or commercial, really ask yourself what type of money are you looking to get from your rental property. Are you looking for a hobby that may produce you with an extra $500-$1,000 a month, then maybe buying a single-family or duplex may be all you need. If you are looking for an opportunity where there is no limit to the potential earnings you can have, perhaps multi-family or commercial is where you need to be looking.

Local or Long Distance

You can have a rental property next door to your house or it could be on the other side of the country, the choice is up to you. It is very convenient having your rental property only 10 minutes down the street. However, is that convenience more important to you then possibly making more money buying in a better market? This is called buying in an appreciating market. Normally this would be ideal, but you may have to look further distances from where you live to accomplish this goal. In this case you may have to hire a property manager. Often times if the market goes up your monthly returns go down with a bigger payout at the end. Also, smaller towns have a tendency to have lager monthly returns but don't appreciate as well.

Self vs Property Management

If you think customers at a shopping center are bad, imagine having a customer that lives in a house that your own. . . they are there 365 days a year and have your cell number. You need to keep this in mind because you will be the one they call at 3:00 in the morning because they decided to flush their dinner down the toilet, and they cannot unclog it. Yes, this has happened, and no, I've never heard of anyone else ever flushing left over food down the toilet. My point is, people do weird things and you need to make sure you are really up for the task if you plan on self-managing the rental. You will save money by not hiring a property manager, which is really the only upside for this road. However, it may be worth the money to not have the headache of your phone ringing from difficult tenants all the time. You will need to hire someone with whom you can trust.

Property Demographics/Location

This may be one of the most important parts to look at. Make sure you look into how the neighborhood looks. Is the neighborhood kept up? What are the people like living next door and in the area? Are there you or old people living there? What size is the house and lot? What are the schools like in the area? Is there a demand for rental property there? If all the answers to these questions fall into what you are looking for then you need to look to see if the amount you would need to lease the property can match the demographics of the area. You are generally looking for properties with good schools, a good neighborhood, smaller and cheaper houses, ones that are not overly updated, maybe in a cul-de-sac, and on a quiet street with a fenced backyard.

Are You Paying Cash or are You Financing?

Again, you will need to know what you are looking to get from a rental property to answer this question. If you have $100,000 and only want to have one rental it may make more sense for you to put more money down. However, if you are looking to create some sort of lifestyle for real estate then perhaps you would benefit more from leveraging that $100,000 and putting a down payment on multiple houses. Here is a basic example for both of these paths below:

House 1 – Purchased with cash

Purchase Price: $100,000

Rent: $1,000 a month

Escrow, Taxes (1%), and insurance (.5%) = $1,500 a year ($125 a month)

Monthly Cash Flow: $875

House 2 – Investment 20% down (numbers pulled from mlcalc.com)

Purchase Price: $100,000

Down Payment: $20,000

Rent: $1,000 a month

Escrow, Taxes (1%), and Insurance (.5%) = $1,500 a year ($125 a month)

Interest Rate: 4.5%

Mortgage (includes Escrow): $506 a month

Principle: $131 a month

Cash Flow: $506.36

Keep in mind that when you own less then 4 houses you need 20% down. When you own more than 4 houses you need to put down 25%. You can also leverage your initial investment to buy more houses, but we will get into this in another chapter.

Budgeting for Maintenance

Is the house new or old? What are the lifetime repairs while you own the property? For example, builder grade material does not have a lifespan as long as most utilities. New homes are usually build with builder grade A/C units, which only have a life expectancy of 7-10 years. Most people don't move out of a new home before this, so if the house is only 10 years old you may want to check out the A/C unit. If it needs to be replaced it may run you $3,000-$6,000 depending on where you live in the country. Roofs are another expense that can cost you between $10,000-$15,000 to replace. Roofs tend to last 20-25 years if installed correctly. Long story short, run your numbers and make sure you have a budget for repair expenses.

Have an Exit Plan

You need to know how long you want to keep the property. Is the home going to be part of your retirement? Did you buy the house at the bottom of the market and just want to hold onto it till the next boom? Either way have a plan. You can always change plan A, just follow plan A until you have plan B in place. If you change the plan, make sure you run the number again if needed. Always have a plan to possibly sell the house if needed.

Additional Thoughts to Keep in Mind

-Keep in mind the goal is to buy a property that is cash flow positive from day one, which means your rent is more than the monthly expanses.

-Nothing ever goes perfectly with a rental home. There are just too many variables.

-You don't lose till you sell.

-Always remember that it is a business and needs to be run as one.

-Nobody will care about the house as much as you do. Tenants will never take care of the house as well as you would like them to.

-Make sure you have an extensive lease written up. Do not skip this step.

-Tax advantages are a perk.

2 BUILDING ON THE BASICS

So now that you have gone over basic features that can make your property profitable we need to look a little further into some of the details. Anyone can drive into a neighborhood, look at a few houses on the same street, do a quick walk through of a house and come to a quick decision on whether it has potential to be profitable. However, if this is a property you are looking to keep long term then you may need to look a little deeper and ask a few more questions.

Below I am going to expand on some ideas mentioned in chapter 1 as well as adding some new ideas to think about when searching for your first rental property.

Neighborhood

I touched on this a little in the first chapter, but I really want to make sure this information is not overlooked. The reason for this is the neighborhood will not only influence the type of renters you will attract, but will also influence how often you will have vacancies. For example, if you have a property near a college or university you may attract renters that are looking for only a twelve-month lease at best. Most college students return home in the summer and may only want to sign a month to month lease. If you have a property near in the middle of nowhere that is only close to a couple summer camps, you may find it hard to rent out that property for more than three months at a time. The point I am trying to make here is you want renters that are looking to stay long term. If you give renters a reason to stay for multiple years, then you don't have to spend time looking for new tenants. Let's dig into a few more reasons to help find these long-term tenants.

Schools

Always remember that there are people who have no desire to buy or own their own house. Renting is easier to help set a budget then owning a house simply because the owner is the one who pays to fix unexpected thing that break over the years. I bring this up because people with families will be looking to rent in an area where they can send their kids to school. If you find a property near a good school you are opening the door to invite another group of renters to be interested in your rental property. Schools can affect the value of your investment in both a positive way or a negative way. Schools can both affect how much you can rent out your property for and how much you can sell the property for if that time were to come.

Crime

If you find a great deal, that you just can't say no to, but the area breeds criminal activity, the quality of tenants you will be looking at will not be of the highest quality. What exactly do I mean by that? Generally speaking, the people who are looking to live in an area of high crime are either criminals or people that don't have any money to live anywhere else. If you don't mind the criminal activity than by all means have at it. Unfortunately you won't be making any money because the rent will be pennies. On the other side, if the tenants don't have any money then you are just setting yourself up for running around at the beginning of every month for your rent check. It would be in your best interest to go check out the police and/or public records for accurate crime statistics for the area. Don't waste your time asking the homeowner you are buying the property from, because they are going to say whatever they need to in order to get the sale. Same thing with the neighbors, they are not going to tell you they are criminals or are only living there because they can't afford to live anywhere else. Types of criminal activity you are looking to avoid are vandalism rates, petty crimes, serious crimes and whether activity is growing or slowing down. Police presence in the area may also be a good indicator of higher criminal activity.

Amenities

Renters like having everything they need within a short distance. Remember, we live in a microwave society. If we have to drive more than 10 minutes to the grocery store then it's too far. They can find a place to rent that is closer. So the more amenities that are within that 10-15 minute distance the more people will be interested in your property. Some common places to look for are daycare, gyms, grocery stores, malls, movie theaters, parks, playgrounds, restaurants, school, or any other public recreational area that people like to go to. If you are in a city than ask yourself these questions: Are you close to downtown? Is there public transportation? If you are looking in an area that is known for a particular style of life than make sure your rental can help with this. For example, if that area is known for its recreational boating life, you might want to find a property that has a driveway that is big enough for a boat. If the area is known for it nightlife than look for a property that is close to where everyone goes at night there. You can usually find promotional information in the areas of the cities or towns that attracts the most people. This can give you an idea of where the best mix of public amenities and properties can be found.

Job Market

Areas with growing employment opportunities generally attract more people, which leads to more tenants. Things to look at are a new major company is coming to the area. This will surely bring in a wave of people to the area. However, depending on the corporation and type of company this could affect they price of the house, which could affect how much you rent the house for. Look at the company and decide whether they are someone you would want in the area. If they are then tenants will probably too. To find information on the job market in a particular area you can visit the local library or go to the U.S. Bureau of Labor Statistics.

Property Taxes

Taxes are not to be overlooked. Keep in mind that communities now have Community Development District fees (CDD) that tie these fees into your taxes now. Most people are familiar with Home Owners Association fees (HOA) but not CDD. Generally speaking if you have an HOA you can pay monthly, quarterly or yearly, however they are not tied into your taxes. If you miss a payment they just keep sending you notices that you missed a payment and they may be subject to additional late fees. CDD fees, on the other hand, are paid with your taxes. This means if you miss a payment (when you pay your taxes) it's the same as not paying your taxes any you end up with a lien on your house. Besides the mortgage, the taxes are the next biggest expense out of your annual profits. High taxes can mean a nicer area to live in which tends to draw in renters looking to stay long-term. Keep in mind that this isn't always the case, however, it is something to keep in mind. The town's assessment office or tax collector site will have the tax records for you to look at and compare them over the last few years.

A quick note since we brought up HOA and CDD fees is there are usually more rules to follow in communities with these fees. The communities have these rules to help keep the neighborhood(s) looking nice and keeping the value of the homes up. However, if you have a tenant that does not like to follow these rules then the HOA and CDD managers will fine the home owner. Now, if the renter doesn't want to follow the rules, good luck getting them to pay the fine. You will end up evicting the tenants and losing rent while you search for new tenants.

Other Listings and Vacancies in the Neighborhood

You should be looking in the neighborhood for other properties that are being rented out. Not necessarily from a competition standpoint (although that is important), but to give you an idea on whether your property would be worth the purchase. If there is an unusually high number of listings and vacancies in the neighborhood then there are one of two things going on. One would be a seasonal cycle for places near a university, like mentioned earlier, or two, the neighborhood has taken a turn for the worst and people are looking to get out. Of course, if the neighborhood has taken a turn for the worst then walk away, however if its seasonal then you need to make sure you can cover the expenses during the off time. Vacancies can also give you an idea on how high you can set your rent for. Increased vacancy rates will drive monthly rent down from landlord's trying to quickly fill open rentals. Fewer vacancy rates can cause landlords to raise rental rates from demand being higher than the supply.

Rental Rates

Since your rental income will mostly determine whether you have a successful rental property or not, you need to do your research to see what the going rate is in the area. If the average rate in the area is not enough to cover the expenses of your property then you need to keep looking. Your research needs to be thorough enough to tell where the neighborhood will be headed over the next five years. Make sure to consider this, just because you can afford the property now and are making money from the property now doesn't mean you can still make money off of the rental in five years. This can be a very long and boring process if you don't know the area that well, but it could save you from going bankrupt a few years after you buy the home.

Natural Disaster Areas

Hurricanes and flooding in the southeast, tornados in the Midwest and earthquakes and forest fires on the west coast can really scale up your insurance costs. If you live in these areas then you already know what to expect, but if you are not from these areas the price of insurance could catch you off guard. For example, around 2005 sinkholes started to pop up all over Florida more than usual. It started happening enough where the insurance companies decided to offer sinkhole insurance in addition to the home insurance that you already carried. I remember buying a home in Florida around 2009 and my insurance was around $1,500.

This was just a standard home owner's insurance policy. However, if I wanted to get sinkhole insurance on top of the $1,500 it was going to be an extra $2,000 a year. Keep in mind, if you opt-out of sinkhole insurance and a sinkhole-forms under your house, it could cost you between $20,000-$60,000 to fix the house, and not to mention the value of your home just got cut in half (which you have to declare when you sell your house). You don't have to avoid these area, just be mindful of them.

Future Development in the Area

The municipal planning department will have all the information on any new development that is scheduled or has been zoned in your area. If the planning department is showing new business parks, condos or malls going up in the area, it's probably pointing towards good growth in the area. Again, depending on the type of development scheduled to begin, it does have potential to hurt your rental property income. If a popular activity-friendly park is being removed in order to put that business park it may drive locals out. Also, adding additional condo or new housing could increase your competition.

3 WHAT YOU NEED TO HAVE IN PLACE

Let's step away from focusing on the physical aspects of what a rental property needs to have in order to be potentially successful and focus on more of the financial and personal responsibility side of the investment. On paper, the idea of investing in a rental property sounds great. It's like buying a house, but someone else lives in it paying all the bills. However, after reading the first two chapters I'm sure you are starting to realize that there is quite a bit more that needs to go into it. Remember that it is still a business. A business doesn't produce income without having to feed that investment with money. As the saying goes, "It takes money to make money." The saying has never been so true as in the real estate industry. Are there properties out there that will take little investment to produce a consistent income, absolutely, but this is not the norm.

Below are some tips and ideas for buying your first rental property:

Make Sure It's for You

Ask yourself these things: Can I fix things? If so, are you willing to stop what you are doing to go fix an issue for your tenants? It could be as simple as the toilet is clogged, or the food disposal is not working. If you consider yourself handy then you need to ask yourself if you want to put the time in to fix any issues that come up. If you are not handy or don't want to put the time in fixing issues, then you need to ask yourself if you are ok with having the additional expense of paying a property manager to resolve these issues.

Also, keep in mind that when you purchase your first rental property there will be a learning curve. No matter how many books you read about the industry, you cannot know everything going in. Although I try to make this investment as easy as possible by writing this book, it is not realistic for me to write every possible issue or scenario out for you with a solution. As with any new endeavor you will have to figure out what works for you and what does not, along with what you can and cannot do.

Consider Paying Off Your Debt First

If you have debt, then you are committed to those bills first and foremost. If you are starting out in real estate then you don't want to add to your financial stress by adding more bills, because a $10,000 new roof (that was unexpected) can put quite a financial burden on a family. To be perfectly honest, this burden is really an unnecessary one as well. Student loans and medical bills need to get paid off first. If you look at your finances you can probably figure out how to pay these bills off in just a couple years. Rental properties are always going to be in demand, which is why you should wait till you have less debt to get started.

Keep in mind that a rental property would be great way to pay for a child's college expenses. Actually, this is exactly how my father paid for my college. My father was a builder so he was able to build the rental property himself with money he already had. For this reason, his only expenses were taxes and insurance. He kept $200 of the $1200 in rent for these expenses and I was able to put $1,000 a month in the bank to pay for tuition and books each semester (instate tuition). He still collects this rental income to this day. Try to get this started while they are entering high school so if there is a issues you have everything running smoothly when they are entering college.

You Need to Get the Down Payment

Something you may not have known is there is not mortgage insurance with rental properties. Of course, I'm assuming you are not trying to cheat the system and hide your rental property and not pay taxes. This means, you will need a minimum 20% down payment depending on who is willing to lend you the money and what they require. Also, to note, is since you will be claiming this as a rental property you cannot homestead (if your stated offers this) the property and your taxes will be a little to a lot higher.

Be Mindful of Higher Interest Rates

Are interest rates higher than usual right now. Are interest rates showing a steady increase over the last three, six or twelve months? You need to make sure you are getting a low enough interest rate so you can actually turn a profit from your rental property. Something to note, interest rates are usually the lowest and the beginning of each month and the beginning of each quarter. This is due to people wanting to close before the start of the next month, especially builders. Builders are building companies that, just like any other company, have monthly, quarterly and annual sales goals. If a closing gets pushed into the first week of the next month, each day into that month is costing the seller money in tax expenses. Since there is such a big push at the end of the month to close, the interest rates tend to increase a little. Is it fair, no, they are simply taking advantage of the push to close at the end of the month. Usually you get an interest rate locked in for 30-90 days, just make sure if the closing gets pushed back a week or month (i.e. your new construction home is not ready) the closing is not outside that locked in period. So ideally you want to lock in an interest rate at the beginning of the month, quarter and year.

Calculate Your Margins

You have to run the numbers before you make your purchase. It's called having a plan or strategy. Generally speaking you are looking for a "Cap Rate" of around 10%. For the purposed if this chapter you just need to remember your Cap Rate goal is 10%. I will leave the equation below, however, I will be going into this later on in the "Strategies" chapter.

Capitalization Rate = Net Operating Income/Current Market Value (Purchase price)

Maintenance estimates around 1%, plus insurance, HOA/CDD fees, taxes, pest control and landscaping just to name a few. Again, I will get into this in more detail later on.

Do Not Buy a Fixer Upper

There are plenty of properties that are close to, if not, move in ready. Don't be inpatient, take your time and you will find this type of property. Remember, you are trying to keep your expenses down, especially on your first house. There are people who have access to contractors that will work for cheap, but that's usually a family member or someone who provides that contractor with quite a bit of consistent work, which is why they will lower their costs a little. If you have no experience with working with contractors then chances are they you give you a high the normal price, because they know you are new to the industry and will try to take advantage of you. This is an industry where nobody knows for sure where their next paycheck is going to come from. If someone can squeeze an extra $1,000 or more out of you, they will. It's better to search for a house that is priced below market value that needs minor repairs.

Start with a Low-Cost Home

To simplify this, the bigger the house the more it will cost you to maintain it. Although a house with a pool might attract more renters, the monthly expenses of maintaining the pool may not be worth it in the long run. Yes, you can bump up your lease to cover these additional expenses, but just like anything with water or moving parts, they do break down frequently and repairs can add up. Also, things like multiple pitches in the roof or breaks in the roof line can add additional cost when replacing the roof. Houses with porches and docks, or screened in patios will, at some point, require maintenance and repairs. These are all nice things that renters look for, but keep in mind they will cut into your profits. Most experts would suggest you start with a home around $150,000.

You Need to Find the Right Location

I can't emphasize location enough. Look for properties with high amenities like mall, parks, restaurants and theaters. You want a good job market, with low crime rates and low property taxes. If you are in a suburb type area than make sure the school districts are above average. The area will dictate your tenants. The better the tenants the better experience you will have.

Know What Your Operating Expenses Are

Let me just get your mind started on numbers before we dive into this later on. Your overall expenses, on a new property, will between 35%-80% of your gross operating income. Please note that gross is what your profits are before taxes are deducted. You need to shoot for what we call a

50% rule. This means your overall expenses are 50% of your lease, therefore, your profits are at 50%.

Try to Determine Your Return

To compare rental property returns to other investments, stocks will usually offer a 7.5% return and bonds will produce around 4.5%. You need to figure out what your return will be for every dollar you invest. Again, we will be going into these figures a little later, but a good return, on your first house, is around 6% and should increase each year after that. This is why I suggested starting early in your child's high school years.

4 KEYWORDS AND FORMULAS

Terminology and Their Formulas

Cash Flow Formula takes into account property payments, which is good to use if you are going to finance the property. It can tell you the monthly and annual profit from the property, and is a good indication of a "negative" or "even" cash flow (walk away from both negative/even cash flow). Below is a breakdown of the numbers needed in this formula, followed by the formula at the end.

1-Investment Costs are going to be your home price (cash or down payment), your closing costs (usually 6%-7% of your loan), the inspection and rehab (if needed).

2-Monthly Expenses will equal the following: Your mortgage payment (principle and interest), property taxes, insurance, property management (usually 7%-10% of rent), HOA/CDD fees, maintenance (about 4%-8% of rent), utilities, and vacancies (4%-8% of rent if applicable).

3-Monthly Income will have to be an educated estimate based on what tenants are currently paying (if the property was used as a rental before) or by what nearby rental properties are renting for. You can also consult with a local realtor or property manager. Always go with the lower end of these estimates when putting numbers into your formulas.

4-Calculate Your Cash Flow: Cash Flow = Monthly Income – Monthly Expenses. This number needs to be positive. As I mentioned above, you obviously don't want negative cash flow, but you don't want even cash flow either. Even cash flow means you are breaking even.

Note: If you calculate an extra mortgage payment per year, for a 30 year mortgage, you will pay off the mortgage in 18 years.

Net Operating Income (NOI) Formula does not factor in how the property is paid for. This is a formula to use only when payments and interest rates are not known. It tells the income from a property excluding the expenses. Keep in mind this formula should not be used in place of the cash flow formula above. This is a simple formula to be used in addition to other financial factors or when analyzing multiple real estate investments at once.

1-Add up estimated monthly income and multiply by 12 (Monthly income X 12 = Annual Income).

2-Add up monthly expenses (same as in Cash Flow Formula) and multiply by 12 (Excluding mortgage payments).

3-Deduct expenses from Income to get NOI (Annual Income – Annual Expenses = Annual NOI.

Higher NOI usually results in a higher property value.

Capitalization Rate (Cap Rate) Formula is one of the most common metrics used to measure the profitability of a real estate investment. It illustrates the rate of return of a rental property without using the method of financed. It can help you measure the level of risk or show you if the property would be a good investment in a growing market even if it shows a poor Cap Rate now. It doesn't, however, appreciation/depreciation or again include the method of financing.

1-In general the Cap Rate should be around 10% ranging from 8%-12%. This percentage varies given the location.

2-Higher Cap Rates equal higher cash flow, which means you are looking for investments with high Cap Rates

3-Capitalalization Rate = MOI/Current Market Value

Ex. NOI (10,000) with a cost of $1M will have a Cap Rate of 10%

Cash on Cash Return (CoC) is an indicator of how well an investment is doing. This can help you predict future cash flow returns, measure the relationship between cash invested and the cash flow. It can also help you calculate your annual return on investment.

1-All cash purchases will have the same CoC and Cap Rate values unless financed.

2-CoC will always include financing, closing costs and rehab.

3-COC = Annual NOI/Total Cash Investment

4-CoC, which is also called Equity Dividend Rate, is similar to a ROI formula.

Current Market Value Formula is just an additional formula for analyzation purposes.

1-Current Market Value = Capitalization Rate/NOI

Below are some other key numbers to consider throughout this process:

-50% rule: 50% expenses and 50% cash flow.

-10% of income goes to vacancies and repairs.

-10% of income goes to long-term big projects like roofs and parking.

-65% ARV

5 RESIDENTIAL VS. MULTI-FAMILY

Residential vs. Multifamily are two completely different animals, and you need to know the difference between them both. You might think if you are looking to build a real estate empire the more units the better, but if you are just starting out, it might not be the best choice. Below I will get into the pros and cons of both investments to hopefully simplify the two, thus making your decision a little easier.

Residential

The be perfectly honest, this is the easier investment. Residential is easier to rent, because you are only working with one tenant and only having to resolve those issues leaving you with less work to do. You will have more real estate to choose from. There will be more single residential homes then multi-family units, which means you can get better deals. Residential properties will have more of a pool of renters. They are also cheaper to buy with more exit strategies. This path makes more sense if you are not looking to scale up and are looking for more of a side income. Setting a single home up as a business is a little simpler and only makes sense if you have no desire of scaling up. To really simplify the investment, all you are doing is buying a second home and claiming the rent as income.

Now, if you want to build a portfolio, but are not interested in buying a multi-family property, you go right ahead and do that. Far be it for me to stomp on another's dream. However, you may want to keep some things in mind. For example, if you want to grow your portfolio to 50 homes, then you will need to do 50 different inspections, you will have 50 different locations, with 50 separate loan, and you will have to work with 50 different sellers. You will, most likely, be the property manager until you have purchased 4-5 properties. It makes no sense to hire a property manager with just a couple homes, because that expense will be cutting into you cash flow. You will also be paying for all that mileage driving from one property to another.

Multi-Family

There are definitely some pros and cons to purchasing a multi-family home. Multi-family properties have between 2-4 units. The reason this stops at 4 units, is anything over 4 units is considered commercial. Commercial requires a different set of standards and a different approval process. For the sake of this book, we will be focusing on properties in either the residential or multi-family.

Let's get into the pros of multi-family properties. As strange as it sounds, it can be easier to finance. This is because it's easier for banks to approve your loan when the property consistently generates strong cash flow every month (shown by prior owner). The banks see the likelihood of a foreclosure to be less with apartment buildings, therefore making a better investment giving you a better interest rate. It takes much less time to acquire 50 units then 50 homes, which means you can grow your portfolio in less time. You don't necessarily have to worry about having 1-2 vacancies because you still have other income from other units coming in, and this should be a small percentage of your income. It has a "Lower Cost Per Door", meaning your cash flow should be better per unit compared to a residential property. Management is generally more effective, profitable and just makes financial sense at this point. You pay a property manager a percentage of the monthly income and you don't have to spend any time dealing with the tenants. Improvements done on one unit can increase the value and life of all the units. There is the potential to have more control on expenses. You can adjust rent of the units if indicated. You can also be more operationally efficient with community laundry or internet. Playing with expenses will change depending on the property you purchase, these are just some ideas to give you a perspective on possibilities. One of the biggest benefits is the potential to do more with less. There are more tax breaks and incentives, and it just makes more sense if you are planning on scaling up.

Some of the cons of purchasing a multi-family property are the price. They are usually more expensive. It can be harder to find tenants. These days you can almost rent a house for just a couple hundred dollars more and not have to share a building with anyone. If you opt out of using property managers it will be more work. Keep in mind the more humans you put under one roof, you are simply increasing your chances of someone doing something they shouldn't have.

Commercial

If you are looking into commercial property, most investors will tell you to start with around a 16-unit property. I'm not going to get into this number here, you can look up information about it, or perhaps I will put out a book later on for commercial real estate. I just thought it might give you go-getters a perspective on the different of a multi-family and a starting commercial property. Of course, you can start out with a 6 or 10-unit property, but the numbers point toward 16 for the best return on your investment.

COLE GRAHAM

6 GAME PLAN AND CRITERIA STRATEGIES

In this chapter, we are going to cover a step-by-step game plan for purchasing a rental property, along with some financial ideas. Please keep in mind that these are simply guidelines and that every single purchase is different. You may have to tweak your game plan for each purchase you make, however, don't stray to far from your criteria. Also, keep in mind that financing changes every year. Banks have new loan options and they are constantly changing approval measures. The financing ideas I mention is simply to open your eyes to the options you have out there. It is ultimately up to you to decide what is best for you and possibly your family during this time. Let's dive in.

A Step-By-Step Game Plan

1-Do your homework: Remember you are now an entrepreneur and you are trying to develop a business that is going to provide you with income. The Law of Compensation is another way of saying you get what you put in. The homework is where most of the work is done, and it's the work nobody else sees but you. You need to make decisions on what type of property you want. You need to figure out how much you can afford to invest. You need to go over everything in chapters one and two, such as neighborhood and rent in the area (these two are just examples). Also, have a really good idea on how much of a return you want.

2-Make a plan and develop some criteria: With all the information you have gathered from step 1, you now have all the information you need to develop a plan. The plan is what type of property you are looking for and the criteria is what you use to keep yourself on track and accountable to the goal you have made for yourself. As I mentioned before, every property will be different so look at it this way. Your game plan can change a little, however, your criteria cannot. Make a list for a set criteria that needs to be met to make a purchase. A couple of examples are: how much you can lease the unit for, how much the purchase price needs to be, or how much you can put down. Also, the number of units if it is a multi-family unit.

3-Arrange financing: This needs to be done before you begin to shop. Financing should be part of your criteria, which is why the criteria is done first. I will cover the financing options during the second part of this chapter.

4-Begin shopping: It's always helpful to find an agent who specializes in rental property. As mentioned before, they will know the area and what the property can be rented for. Make sure they have access to MLS and you also have the internet for additional resource's.

5-Make an offer: For all cash or conventional loans, this process isn't any different then purchasing a house. You don't want to show your face, and you need to start low. Now please pay attention to this next statement. You can negotiate the closing costs on a purchase. It seems like everyone knows this, but very few every bring it up. For example, in Florida the seller covers most of the closing costs, and the buyer is responsible for their agent along with a couple other small costs. This can be a big advantage if you are looking to purchase a rental property in Florida. However, every state is different, and these can be negotiated. Meaning you will have less out of pocket at closing putting more money into your pocket for rehab or just a reserve fund.

6-Do your due diligence: Do not be cheap on the inspection. If they person expecting the property can test for something, have them test for it. It's better to spend the extra hundred bucks to check termites or moisture then to find out there is an issue later on that costs you $5,000 to repair. Moisture is a huge issue in the northers states, specifically with the drainage piping for the foundation. That's right, the foundation. There isn't as much of a problem with this in newer homes, but always check the moisture of the foundations with homes over 20 years old. If the property is currently being used as a rental, try to see if you can get income records from the current owner. If he gives them to you great, if not, maybe there is a reason to be concerned.

7-You are now a Landlord: It's time for you to make it work

Additional ideas to keep in mind:

1-If you, the landlord, pays some of the expenses (lawn, internet) you will be able to claim higher gross income, which may help you later qualify for additional mortgages.

2-The banks industry standard is two years of Schedule E income from tax returns, meaning you have to show two years' worth of income rental income to claim this as income. Again, being able to obtain previous income claimed by the prior landlord can help you out here.

3-Banks will sometimes allow you to count 75% of your income, from your first property, toward your second property. Let's break this down, .75 X .43 = .3225 (.43 being your debt-to-income ratio), which is about 1/3. This will show your current rental income divided by 3 is the additional monthly debt service that the bank will possibly allow your new rental income to support. Your debt-to-income ratio is a measure of your new and existing monthly debt you currently have compared to your monthly income. It is used to also measure your personal financial leverage you can do. The banks will allow a ratio as high as 43% (which is where we got .43 in the equation above) on owner occupied multi-family properties. All this means is the mortgage payment can be up to 43% of that income if you have no personal debt. Real estate is an industry where leveraging your income and assets is much more expectable and there are many avenues to do this. Please check out the graphs on page 94 and 95 at the end of the book that illustrates this idea.

4-If you can have well documented rental history for the new property you are about to purchase, the banks may take that into consideration as well.

5-Keep in mind that the more personal expenses you have, when starting out, the more you will be limited on how much you can borrow.

6-I mentioned this earlier, always have exit strategies. This means being able to sell or somehow change the initial game plan if the income is not coming in. You must be able to pay the monthly debt or be able to sell if needed. Besides selling you can refinance, ad a partner, find a long term private investor, or flip it.

7-I don't usually suggest this, but it is an option. If you are needing repairs and don't have the funds you can always look for credit cards that have promotion of no interest for 12-18 months. Just remember that when you go this route it will be another company that you must pay each month. I would look for private lenders, that won't show on your credit and may be able to work with you if you need to miss a month.

7 FINANCING OPTIONS

Financing can get a little confusing. I am going to attempt to give you the most common means of obtaining financing that investors use. Again, things will change as time goes on, a few of these options may not be available in the future, and some new options will be available. Also, some of the percentages may change, but they should still be in the ballpark. I will start with the easiest to understand followed by the most common and so forth.

All Cash

Of course this is the most ideal, but also impossible means of financing, especially when you are just starting out. The biggest benefits of an all cash purchase are you don't pay any interest, and your cash flow will be higher. Only about 24% of investors in the US use cash to finance an investment. However, if you are planning on having multiple investment properties, you may choose to leverage your cash investment. Instead of putting down all cash on one property, you may choose to put 20% down on five different properties, thus increasing your cash flow.

Example:

Eric has $100,000 to invest in a property. Eric purchases a $100,000 house, all cash. If Eric rents out the property for $1,000 a month he will yield a 12% return on investment.

If Eric decided to leverage that $100,000 as 20% down payment on five properties all purchased for $100,000. With an $80,000 mortgage on each unit and each unit rented out at $1,000, you will have a cash flow of $300 for each unit. Multiplying $300 by five units equals $1,500 per month or $18,000 return on investment, which is a 50% increase over the initial all cash purchase.

Conventional Mortgage

Most investors choose to finance their properties with a traditional conventional mortgage. The reason for this is due to the example above. If you plan on scaling up to multiple properties then you can and should take advantage of leveraging your cash. Most conventional mortgages require a minimum of 20% down, however these down payments can increase to 25-30%. This all depends on the lender and the type of property. Conventional mortgages will generally provide the lowest interest rates.

FHA Loans

The Federal Housing Administration (FHA) is a US government program that insures mortgages for banks. Getting this type of loan puts insurance on your mortgage similar to having car insurance or health insurance. One of the rules is that the homeowner must live in the house that this loan is taken out for. The way around this rule is you are still able to buy a duplex or a 3-4-unit investment property, you just have to live in it. The biggest benefit of an FHA loan is the low-down payment. When these loans first came out the down payment was 3%, and is now at 3.5%. However, remember that insurance I was talking about? The FHA loan requires that you pay for that insurance called "Private Mortgage Insurance" (PMI). This insurance protects the lender and is required with any down payment of less than 20%. This additional payment will be added to your mortgage, which will cut into your cash flow. A rough estimate of this insurance is between $80-$100 for every $100,000 mortgage. You may want to keep in mind that FHA loans require the house to be "move in ready". They don't' want the property to need a new roof, AC, electrical work, etc., since they are taking all the risk.

Portfolio Lenders

First let's get into how conventional loans work so you can better understand what portfolio lenders are. You can get conventional loans from banks, credit unions, and mortgage brokers. Most of the time these companies are not using their own capital for the loan, but are simply borrowing the funds from a third party or are going to sell the loan to a company that is backed by the government, such as Fannie Mae and Freddie Mac. They are simply selling the loan to replenish the funds they loaned you. This is the reason for all of the strict rules and guidelines you need to follow and meet in order to get approved for the loan. Some people find it difficult to get approved for conventional loans when the loan is for real estate investments and other self-employed investments.

There are, however, some banks and credit unions that can and will give loans from their own funds. This is what makes them a portfolio lender. With the money being their own, they are able to give loans with more flexibility with the rules and guidelines. Keep in mind that most of these banks and credit unions don't advertise that they are portfolio lenders, so you will have to either ask around or call the company directly to find out.

203K Loans

This loan piggybacks off of the FHA loan, however you are able to purchase the property if the house needs some rehab work. You still have the low-down payment of 3.5% (current rate), but this loan gives you the advantage of putting those rehab costs right into the loan itself. You still need to live at the property and it can be used on duplexes, and 3-4-unit properties. They will also be adding that PMI as they do with an FHA loan.

Home Equity Loans and Lines of Credit

This is simply using the equity in your primary home to finance your investment property. Banks and Investment Companies use services, such as, Home Equity Installment Loan (HEIL), and Home Equity Line of Credit (HELOC) they use to give access to this equity to the home owner. Of course, you need equity in your home to use this service and banks typically only lend up to a certain percentage of the home's value. Every bank and company is different but you can get up to 90% of the value of your home minus what you owe. Some benefits of using this loan are the banks generally do not look at the property you are looking to invest in. Since the line of credit comes from your primary house, the primary house is all they are concerned about. The line of credit comes in the form of cash and you are free to do with is as you please. This includes the ability to have a cash closing, which makes you more likely to get the property over someone who needs to finance. Some lines of credit can have tax benefits. The interest rate is typically lower then Hard or Private Money. These types of loan can also come with fixed and adjustable interest rates so make sure you stick to the criteria you set to make sure this is a good option for you.

Owner Financing

Basically what this means is the person selling the house to you is willing to just have you pay them monthly payments instead of you going through a bank. In order for this to happen the owner/seller owns the property free and clear. If you choose this option, please make sure the seller owns the house and does not have a mortgage on the house. If they still have a mortgage then they do not own the house. With almost every purchase of a property you sign a clause called the "Due on Sale" clause, which means the prior lender has the right to request complete payment of the loan once the house is sold. There are investors who ignore this clause and take the risk. On the flip side, you may wish to use this option when you go to sell your property.

Private Money

This type of financing is similar to "Hard Money", but the big difference is the lender does not do this as a profession. Usually the lender has some sort of prior relationship with the borrower and is looking to simply get some type of return on their current cash on hand. Since there tends to be a prior relationship before the transaction, the terms are more flexible and the fees are less. These terms that are usually set in this type of financing are a set interest rate, their investment is usually secured with a promissory note and mortgage on the property. Meaning if the borrower doesn't pay them the lender can foreclose on the house. All these terms are agreed to prior to the money being lent and the agreed time of the loan can be anywhere from 6 months to 30 years. One benefit of this type of financing is the interest rate is based on the money borrowed, which means if you can increase rent or the value in the property goes up you are able to pay back the lender quicker.

Note: When you use Hard Money or Private Money the most important thing to realize is the need to establish reliability and credibility with these types of lenders. If you fail to honor your work or pay back one of these lenders on time, your name will spread quickly and it will be harder to get loan in the future this way. On the flip side, if you continue to meet the terms and these lenders continue to make money off of the loan they provided for you they are more likely to continue loaning you money as needed.

Hard Money

This is financing that is acquired from an individual or private business for the only purpose of investing in real estate. One this that separates this type of financing from the rest are the specific characteristics of the terms it has. The term lengths of the loan are usually shorter (6-36 months) and the loan is usually based of the value of the property. The interest rates are usually higher between 8-15%, including higher fees to get the loan. The lenders of the loan typically do not require income verification or credit references. They load does not show on your credit report, and can you can usually have the funds within a few days. The lenders are also a little more understanding when properties need rehab. These types of loans are good in situation that require just a short period, however, investors can and do run into trouble when the loan runs out. You need to make sure you have multiple exit strategies when utilizing this type of loan. You can find these lenders by asking real estate agents, house flippers, looking in the newspaper, Craigslist, online or a mortgage broker.

Partnership

Partnership is a very loose term because there are some many ways this partnership can be made. So, to simplify the term, it is exactly what is says and that is a partnership. You are bringing in another person to help close the deal. The terms will be decided between the partners because there are no set rules. The added partner can have an active or passive role. The added partner can be just as involved as the initial investor, as far as hands on work, or simply provide financing. Usually these investors are looking for a percentage of the initial investors cash flow. This means a cut in the cash flow, appreciation, depreciation and profit from selling the property. There is typically not agreed interest rate on the initial investment from the added partner, it's simply from what the property generates. The added partner usually takes on more risk than other lenders, but have the opportunity to make much more.

Commercial Loans

As I mentioned earlier, any property with more than four units is considered commercial. Commercial loans usually have a little higher interest rates and fees, different standards to qualify and shorter-term limits. When financing a commercial property there is one big difference on how you get qualified. Instead of the banks looking at the amount of money the borrower makes, which is how you qualify for a conventional loan, the bank looks at how much revenue the property generates. The reason for this is the borrower is probably not going to be able to cover a mortgage payment on a multi-million-dollar commercial property, so they have to look at the possible revenue the property can make to make sure they get their payment every month. Not to say they won't send you through the same proof of income as does a conventional loan, but it's not a realistic comparison. One big benefit to commercial loans it the ability for the lender to extend a business line of credit for other real estate investments, like flipping houses.

Crowdfunding and REITs

I'm not going to get into these, because I don't have much experience with it, but I felt I needed to add it because it is a form of investing in properties. In a nut shell, it is a simply way of putting $1,000 or less down on an investment property. The idea is multiple people do this, it is completely passive, you get a percentage back, and you have very little control of the investment. If you would like more information I'm sure you can find it on-line or on investment websites (REIT.com, www.realityshares.com, fundrise.com).

As I mentioned above, there is no way to cover every possible financing option available and some of these will not be available, depending on when you are reading this. You cannot do enough research on financing options available. With the more experience you obtain, as you build your portfolio, the more creative you will become with financing. However, you cannot become creative without knowing the basics, and that's what I have gone over above.

8 HOW TO INCREASE THE VALUE OF YOUR INVESTMENT PROPERTY

If you are not maximizing the potential of your rental property then you are leaving money on the table. There are a number of things that are required for someone to live in a property you own. These are the things you looked for when you were first looking to purchase the property. Now you need to take all these requirements and figure out just how to make the most money out of them. Let's look at what you can do to increase the value of your rental property:

Decrease Expenses

Without decreasing the value of the rental, try and figure out where you can cut expenses, because let's face it, there are a lot of them. You have expenses with accountants, advertising, insurance, lawyers, legal fees, licenses, maintenance, property management and repairs. If you are in a suburban area, competition is high and you can always find people to do these tasks for less than their competitors you just need to look around and you need to do this once a year.

Pass the Expenses to the Tenants

Not only is this one less task or tasks that you need to handle, but leaving cable, internet, electricity (you would need a separate meter for each unit), gas, and water to the tenants can increase the value of your property. These expenses can and usually do increase every year or two. By having the tenants pay for these it may help keep the price of your lease in a position that is more profitable. For one the tenants get exactly what they want and can choose to monitor some of these expanses. This can make the rental more attractive to renters. It may also prevent you from having to increase rent each year. Yes, increasing your rent each year may need to be done if taxes go up or cost of living, but having to also keep up with other expenses increasing may cause you to increase the lease more than what the renters are willing to pay. Thus, making you spend more of your time looking for new tenants.

Raising Rent

Since I mentioned this before, we mine as well get into it next. You want to make sure your rates are at or near market value. You don't have to have your rates less than your competitors if you have more to offer, just make sure you are within a realistic range. A standard inflation rate is 3% a year. I've seen an increase as low at .4% and as high as 4.5%, which just happen to follow one another. Keep in mind that 3% on a $1,000 unit is only $30, but if you have multiple units, this percentage can add up in the long run.

Add-Ons

Maybe one of the units has a garage, or a specific parking spot. There are many rentals that don't allow pets. Keep in mind that pet can and usually do cause more damages then humans do, but it gives you an option to increase the value of your unit. Maybe there are resources that can be shared between all the units (i.e. washer and dryer). This can keep down the expenses in each unit, and possibly prevent the renters from having to purchase their own units.

Repairs and Upgrades

Look to update and modernize outdated units. Outdated units give the impression that little money is going into the property and may turn off renters. Updated properties show that the owner takes pride in what they have and may make the potential renters feel like they will be taken care of while they are renting there. Of course, with an increase of value come an increase of rates. If you really feel like adding some improvement costs you can try adding square footage to the property. Knocking down walls and making an open floor plan makes the rental look bigger. Adding hallway closets and rooms will also allow you to increase your rates with the added value.

Combining and/or Subdividing Units

Sometimes you come across properties that are at a great price, and have a lot of potential but just don't seem to compare to the market around them. That's were doing your homework prior to purchasing comes into play. For example, if you are in an area were multiple families/generations like to live together, then maybe your property with three small units isn't going to work for them. Go back to the chapter that covers repairs and upgrades. Maybe knocking down a wall to combine two units would be more beneficial in the long run. It may drop you down to just two units, but you can increase the rate to make up the loss of the third unit.

Property Taxes

You can try and decreasing your property taxes. This isn't a common tactic, or an easy one for that matter, but it has and can be done. What you need to do is try and show the local property appraiser that the property is not worth what they currently have the property listed at. If the book value of the property is lowered (or just the house on the property) then the taxes will be lowered.

9 RECAP AND SOME EXTRAS

Below are some bullet points to quickly recap what we have gone over so you will be able to apply them into the steps laid out in the next chapter. You will need to go back and reread the information at the beginning, because I would be surprised if anyone can remember every detail. That's why we make criteria.

Do Your Research

Then you do more research followed by more research. Unless you have been at this for a while then you really can't do enough research. There is always something to learn, and you won't learn everything during your first purchase.

You Are Buying Numbers, Not a Property

t's not an emotional investment, it's a financial one. Remember, you are going to have exit strategies in case something goes south. This is not a marriage so don't feel the need to keep it around if it's not working out. During your fist purchase try not to over improve or invest too much time and capital.

Have Criteria

Developing a spreadsheet of some sorts will help you on track and stick to your game plan. It should help you analyze deals, including a fair market value, money down, mortgage, carrying costs, improvements, along with expenses and rental rates, and ending with your cash-on-cash return on your investment.

By Local

By local if you can, however, a better deal is better than buying local

Think Long Term

If you are looking to invest in rental properties then

you need to be thinking long term. If you are looking for the short term, you are just setting yourself up for more unnecessary work. Remember, if you sell a home, then you will need to buy a new one. Yes you will hopefully made some money on your flip (if it's short term then this is essentially what you did) then you have money in the bank, but you no longer have money coming in. If you don't invest that money somewhere else, then all you have is a savings account that will eventually disappear. So, what you will need to do is buy another property. That includes redoing everything you have learned in this book. From what I can tell that's a lot of work for $30,000. Let's make it easy on ourselves and think long term.

Don't Use a Shotgun Approach

Try and bundle your properties together, but no more than two or three areas. Start with one area, develop multiple properties in this area, hire a property manager and once you develop a good relationship with that property manager move into the next area or properties. The last thing you want is to have 3-4 properties in 3-4 different areas. It's too much driving for you, and you don't want to be paying a property manager the travel time.

You Need to Learn to Manage Your Property Manager

If you don't have the temperament to be a property manager then you will need to hire one. Remember that everyone has a different personality. If you want someone to be like you then you will need to find someone with the same personality of your own, because you cannot teach or change this. You can always tell someone where to go and when to go there.

You Need Cash Flow Positive

To simplify this statement, your lease needs to be more than your expenses. Again, do your homework. Nothing is more frustrating than a shotgun purchase, to later find out you can't lease the property for what the expenses are. I think we all would be happy with an investment property, we would never live in, that nets us $600 a month, then a property we love but we only break even. Let's say you didn't do your homework and you need a quick estimate, remember the 1% rule. You take your monthly lease and divide that month by the purchasing price of the house. You ideally would like the percentage to be at or above 1%.

Quality, Quality, Quality

Finally, just make it easy on yourself and don't' be afraid to look at multiple homes to find a quality property that doesn't need a lot of money to get it ready. Patients is the name of the game, and if you do your homework you won't have to wait as long.

10 WHAT YOU NEED TO KNOW BEFORE YOU PURCHASE YOUR FIRST PROPERTY

What I have put together here is a list of common questions I have either thought or questions I've heard from others about what they wish they had known prior to their purchase. Now, everyone is different and what is important to me might not be that important to you, but again, it gets you thinking.

Tenants

You need to be selective when picking your tenants. Now I really do mean selective. You may be excited to get those first tenants in there to start that cash flow, but the wrong tenants can cost you more then you make. Take care of your good tenants once you find some. Don't feel the need to increase the lease every year by the "standard" 3% cost of living increase. I mean, I lived beside an owner who would start a lease out at $1,000 a month and increase it $100 each year, and I would just shake my head. I use to live beside these renters, who were great people, great neighbors, but they would just leave every 1-2 years because the owner kept increasing the rent $100 a year. With the exception of one year, the cost of living never hit 3%. Good renters will cost you less in the long run so don't nickel and dime them.

Property Taxes

Remember, taxes should go up. You need to hope for this and anticipate it. If property taxes are going up then the value of your home and area is going up. Worst case scenario is the taxes go up so high you can't afford to rent the property so you sell if at a higher value then you purchased it. Tax caps are at least 1% higher on rental properties and you cannot homestead them. Just keep this in mind when you are doing your homework at the beginning.

Your Lease Agreement

This is where you set the rules in black and white, and remember, you set them so stick to them. Once you let one rule go the renters will push the envelope as far as they can. If you state there will be late fees on rent checks, then make sure you are charging them late fees, or don't be surprised when you have to go chasing down that rent check.

Don't Be Afraid to Stop by Often

I mean, don't be stopping by multiple times a week, but enough to let them know you are around. You don't want to invade their privacy but you can let them know that you want to make sure they property is taken care of and you may stop by from time to time to do a walk around the house and maybe do a walk through to check on utilities and appliances. While you are checking over all those things you may want to observe the living and sleeping areas for damages along with the ceilings for leaks.

Repairs

Most repairs will be expensive and unexpected. You can possibly minimize this risk if you have good home inspector prior to your purchase. Just keep in mind that most people use all their savings as a down payment and don't have a large emergency fund to start off with. This isn't to scare you, just something to keep in mind when your purchasing that first investment. If possible, plan ahead and save as much of the cash flow as possible till you have a decent size emergency fund. Roofs are generally $10-$15,000, central A/C units are about $6,000, and you know how much utilities are, so what is a good emergency fund? It really depends on your cash flow, but it you have one property and one unit I would go with $10,000. The cost of a roof is more than this, but roofs are usually 20 years and you can plan for the new roof bases off of what the estimated life of the roof is during your inspection.

What Does Time Magazine Think?

There was an article in Time Magazine that had a few suggestions when thinking of purchasing a rental property. Here is what they said:

-You should be handy and like fixing things.

-Warns people who work 60 hours a week with kids to not take on such an investment.

-It's the exception to have everything go well.

-Make sure you have enough savings in case something goes wrong.

-Deals can be found in an increasing market.

-Biggest rookie mistake is underestimating the renovation cost and ongoing maintenance.

11 WHY YOU SHOULD BUY A RENTAL PROPERTY

Of course, the reason why we want to purchase a rental property is to make money, but this isn't just a 9-5 job where you show up to collect a paycheck. This is yours, and it can be as great as you want it to be or it can end up being worth nothing if you let it. I've added below a few other benefits to buying a rental property that you may or may not have thought of.

Retirement Plan

American are terrible savers, and in order for your 401 to be worth anything you have to work until your 65. By purchasing a rental property, it almost forces you into a retirement plan. Think of it this way. You purchase a property at the age of 30 and you have a 30-year mortgage. Let's say the expenses and cash flow are 50/50, at $1,200 a month, with gives you an extra $600 a month. At the age of 60 you will pay off your mortgage and could potentially only have taxes and maintenance on the property if the tenants pay the expenses themselves. I'm guessing that would put you around the $1,000 a month of cash flow.

Leveraging Money

I mentioned before that this is an industry where you can do this with little money. It's pretty impressive with only $100,000 in the bank how fast you can leverage that money. Put five down payments on property and increase your return on investment.

Tax Deferring

This is something that you really need to go over with your financial advisor or accountant so mistakes are not made. In saying that you should be thinking about tax deferred strategies with appreciation over the long term.

Tax Free Cash Flow

You need to start thinking like a business owner when it comes to taxes. Depreciation and mortgage interest deductions, assuming you leveraged your capital, should almost make your cash flow tax free. Many times, investors don't' pay taxes on their cash flow and will wait to pay capital gains when they sell the property later on down the road.

Tax Write-Offs

Many time investors will write off personal expenses a legitimate business deductions such as internet, and vehicles. Again, check with your accountant, but realistically there are many personal expenses that you can write off under your business account. You work from home with this business and just like any other business there are expenses. You know pay for those expenses up front and are allowed to write them off.

COLE GRAHAM

CONCLUSION

I read on <u>Investopedia</u>:

"Rental Property Investing is a preferred strategy for people looking for a second income and can invest in something that will appreciate slowly over time".

Real estate typically has an eight-year cycle were the real estate market will be booming and then quickly drop. It takes about 8 years for the market to build back up. You will need to keep in mind that this cycle has been the same for many years and your property will never be worth nothing. You will have to continue to follow your game plan and remember that the investment is for the long term.

Let's briefly cover the steps to purchase an investment rental property:

Step 1: Do your homework. This is the most time-consuming task and can sometimes be the most repetitive and boring one, but it is the most important. I would even say more important than getting a deal on a property.

Step 2: Set up a game plan and develop some criteria. You have to decided what you want and how you can get that. Once you figure that out, set up some criteria that needs to be met to get it and a long-term game plan to reach your ultimate goal.

Step 3: Arrange financing. Make sure you do this before you start looking, because you really don't know what you can purchase unless you know what you can spend. Make sure you look into more than one option to finance.

Step 4: Begin shopping. There are deals if you are willing to be patient. Again, don't jump on the first home you look at. Find a reliable inspector and let him know what you are looking for and what your criteria is.

Step 5: Make an offer. It never hurts to get a low-ball offer, especially on properties that have been on the market for a while. Remember, you can negotiate with closing costs. It's an investment, nobody will criticize you for trying to get the best price.

Step 6: Do your diligence. If the inspector can test for it, have them test for it. Try to find out if properties in the area are all having issues with something (termites, sinkholes). Any information on the house will help you decide if it is going to be a good investment properties. If you purchase a home and end up with a surprise problem than you didn't do enough research.

Remember to keep an open mind and be optimistic with your rental properties. Some years may be more difficult than others depending on repairs and tenants. You just need to keep a positive attitude, keep your game plan in mind, and remember what you can accomplish in the long run.

RENTAL PROPERTY INVESTING

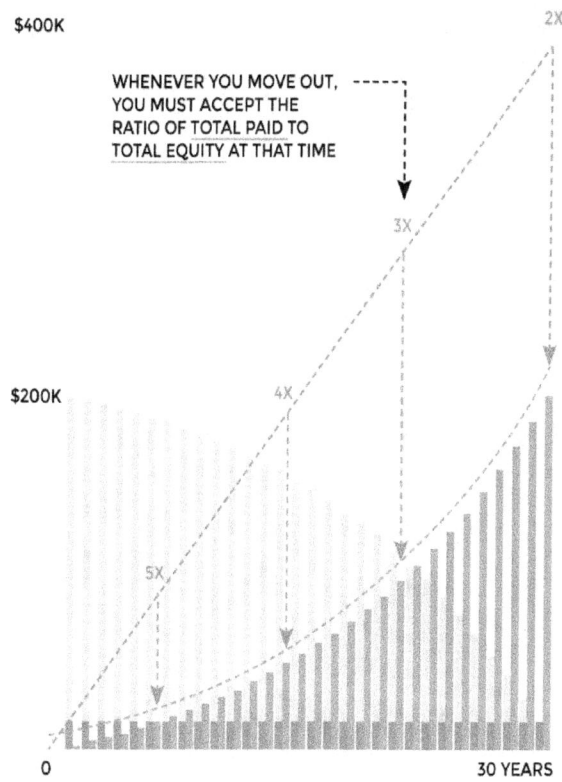

WHENEVER YOU MOVE OUT, YOU MUST ACCEPT THE RATIO OF TOTAL PAID TO TOTAL EQUITY AT THAT TIME

$400K

$200K

0

30 YEARS

2X

3X

4X

5X

Single Family Primary Residence

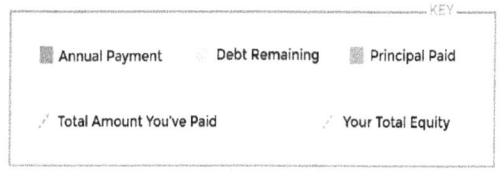

KEY

Annual Payment   Debt Remaining   Principal Paid

Total Amount You've Paid   Your Total Equity

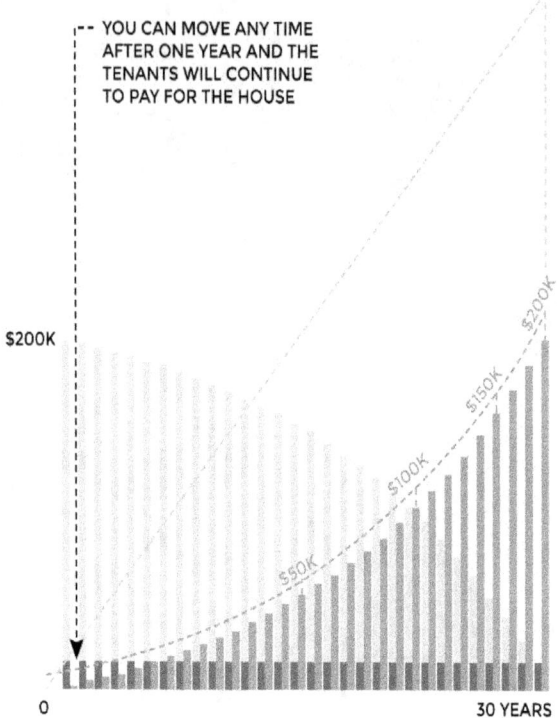

YOU CAN MOVE ANY TIME AFTER ONE YEAR AND THE TENANTS WILL CONTINUE TO PAY FOR THE HOUSE

Small Multifamily Primary Residence

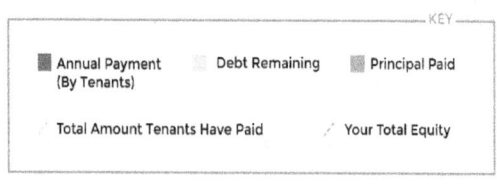

KEY

Annual Payment (By Tenants) Debt Remaining Principal Paid

Total Amount Tenants Have Paid Your Total Equity

ABOUT THE AUTHOR

Cole Graham is a self-taught real estate investor and online marketer. Cole is always looking into other industries to make money; however, he strongly believes that real estate and ecommerce have the most potential and is where he focuses most of his time. Cole believes that real estate and ecommerce, although quite complex, requires just a little knowledge to be able to start making money. He stresses the importance of that knowledge to be the right information, which is why he has felt the need to share his personal education with other go getters. Cole does have a little background with properties, given he grew up working construction with his father. Although he has general knowledge of construction, he would not consider himself an expert in this field. When Cole started out in the real estate industry he thought his knowledge of construction could make up for his lack of knowledge with every other aspect of the industry and he prove to be right. After years of applying his simple methods in real estate, with success Cole tried the same idea with ecommerce, and again found success. Cole truly believes that there are multiple paths for entrepreneurship with unlimited information available for you to use and succeed. Although Cole is still very active in real estate and ecommerce, he now feels the need to share this information with anyone who is looking to break away from the norm and take responsibility of their own financial future.